Career Quest

EXPLORING SPORTS AND FITNESS CAREERS

STEPHANIE LOUREIRO

TWENTY-FIRST CENTURY BOOKS / MINNEAPOLIS

Twenty-First Century Books™
An imprint of Lerner Publishing Group, Inc.
241 First Avenue North
Minneapolis, MN 55401 USA

For reading levels and more information, look up this title at www.lernerbooks.com.

Main body text set in Bembo Std Regular.
Typeface provided by Monotype Typography.

Library of Congress Cataloging-in-Publication Data

Names: Loureiro, Stephanie author
Title: Exploring sports and fitness careers / Stephanie Loureiro.
Description: Minneapolis : Twenty-First Century Books, 2026. | Series: Career quest | Includes bibliographical references and index. | Audience: Ages 11–18 | Audience: Grades 7–9 | Summary: "What do nutritionists do? How do you become a sports coach? Discover the many jobs in the sports and fitness industry in this guide"—Provided by publisher.
Identifiers: LCCN 2025011239 (print) | LCCN 2025011240 (ebook) | ISBN 9798765662717 library binding | ISBN 9798348029562 paperback | ISBN 9798348000028 epub
Subjects: LCSH: Sports—Vocational guidance—Juvenile literature | Physical fitness—Vocational guidance—Juvenile literature | Sports sciences—Vocational guidance—Juvenile literature
Classification: LCC GV734.3 .C367 2026 (print) | LCC GV734.3 (ebook) | DDC 796.023/73—dc23/eng/20250515

LC record available at https://lccn.loc.gov/2025011239
LC ebook record available at https://lccn.loc.gov/2025011240

Manufactured in the United States of America
1 – CG – 12/15/25

CONTENTS

INTRODUCTION ---- 4

CHAPTER ONE
INTRO TO SPORTS AND FITNESS CAREERS ---- 6

CHAPTER TWO
COACHING ---- 12

CHAPTER THREE
FITNESS AND WELLNESS ---- 20

CHAPTER FOUR
THE OTHER SIDE OF SPORTS ---- 35

CHAPTER FIVE
THE FUTURE OF SPORTS CAREERS ---- 49

CONCLUSION
AN INDUSTRY FOR ALL ---- 54

Glossary ---- 56
Source Notes ---- 58
Selected Bibliography ---- 59
Further Information ---- 60
Index ---- 62

INTRODUCTION

You wake up and get ready to head out the door for your college team's soccer practice. Before you leave, you make sure to eat a healthful, balanced breakfast that the team nutritionist recommended to you. During practice, your strength and conditioning (S&C) coach has the team running drills. You start to notice you feel a little off. Your right ankle—the one you had surgery on a few months ago—feels irritated when you run. On top of that, your mind is all over the place and can't focus.

After practice is over, you talk to the head coach to let them know what's going on. Then you head to see the team's physical therapist. The physical therapist checks your ankle and makes sure it is still recovering well. The therapist also gives you some exercises and stretching routines you can do at home to help it feel better.

Next, you decide to knock on the door of the team psychologist. You let the psychologist know that you've been feeling unfocused and having trouble bouncing back mentally from your surgery. You've been feeling more anxious and less

More than 522,000 students in the United States compete in a sport at their college or university. More than 8,000,000 high school students play at least one sport.

confident. You and the psychologist schedule an appointment to discuss it.

Your day as an athlete is filled with people in all kinds of careers—nutritionists, coaches, therapists, and psychologists. All these careers, while dealing with very different aspects of the field, are part of the sports and fitness industry.

CHAPTER ONE

Intro to Sports and Fitness Careers

When you hear "sports and fitness careers," what is the first thing that comes to mind? You might think of a professional athlete such as a baseball player or a soccer player. Or maybe you think about a coach for a professional sports team. While athletes and coaches are a major part of the industry, there's much more to sports and fitness than playing and coaching sports. In fact, there are careers in sports and fitness that you have probably never even thought of.

What Is the Sports and Fitness Industry?

Sports and fitness are major fields around the world. Technically two fields in one, they cover everything from commercial gyms to sports marketing to personal trainers to professional team owners. Research company Research and Markets says, "The global sports market reached a value of nearly $484.9 billion in 2023." And in the United States alone, the fitness industry is worth $40 billion.

The sports side of the industry includes professional athletes, athletic scouts, sports journalists, announcers, referees, and analysts. On the fitness side, careers include personal trainers, physical therapists, strength coaches, and gym owners. However, sports and fitness are not wholly separate entities. They often go hand in hand. As a result, you will often find that a career in sports can fit into or overlap a career in fitness and vice versa.

Announcers and sports analysts are important parts of the professional sports industry. They provide fans watching on television with a better understanding of what's happening during a game.

Professional Athletes

Being a professional athlete is more than just fun and games. It takes dedication and a lot of hard work. Professional athletes not only have a deep love for their sport of choice, but they are also disciplined. They work and train through every up and down whether they want to or not. Training to become a professional athlete requires not only immense physical skill but also mental skill as well. Discipline, confidence, resilience, and a strong desire to succeed are key traits to have if you want to be a professional athlete.

Becoming a professional athlete does not require any specific education or degree. Most professional athletes are recruited during their college years and are asked to join a professional team once they've graduated. Because of this, most professional athletes start playing their sport and training

Playing on a professional team is one of hundreds of jobs in the sports and fitness field.

when they are young, often in high school or even earlier. During high school, they hope to be scouted for a college team. Then after high school, they attend college and play for that team in the hopes of being scouted or recruited for a professional team.

Athletes spend hours of their days practicing and preparing for their games and events. They might spend extra time analyzing their sport and their performance, getting in extra workouts, or reading books on how to become better, more focused athletes.

Being an aspiring pro athlete sometimes means having to do things when you don't want to do them. Everyone has days when they would rather not do something—no matter how much they love it. When a person is training to become a professional athlete, the option to stop or take a few days off is often not an option. These athletes spend years, and often most of their lives, training to become the best of the best. Being a pro athlete means being dedicated, even when you're not motivated.

For some people, having a bad day or a performance or practice that felt subpar might be enough to make them want to stop or take a break. Aspiring professional athletes often don't have that option either. They develop and practice mental skills to help them push past obstacles. Athletes use techniques such as visualization, self-talk, and meditation to strengthen their mindset. Simone Biles, the most decorated gymnast of all time, was caught on camera at the 2024 Paris Olympics muttering to herself, "You got this. It's your time," before a balance beam performance. It just goes to show that even the greatest athletes psych themselves up and remain dedicated.

College Degrees in Sports and Fitness

Many careers in sports and fitness require college degrees, experience, or a mix of both. Here are ten of the most common undergraduate degrees found within the industry:

- kinesiology: the study of how the body moves and how physical fitness affects overall health
- parks and recreation management: the study of how to develop and manage recreational activities and park resources
- coaching: the study of how the human body works, how to improve athlete performance and well-being, and behavior in sports and exercise
- sports analytics: the study of how to collect, analyze, and use data to make decisions within the sports industry
- sports media: the study of broadcasting and reporting sports in mass media
- sports journalism: the study of reporting, interviewing, and writing about sports news and related events
- event management: the study of planning and executing various events such as conferences and concerts, as well as inner workings of stadiums such as concessions, ticketing, and marketing
- photography: the study of photography covering composition, editing, history, and techniques
- public relations: the study of using communication strategically to build and maintain positive relationships between organizations and clients such as athletes and celebrities
- sports broadcasting: the study of how to analyze and communicate sports information and events to the public using various media

More than Athletes

While athletes play a major role in the sports and fitness industry, there are several more careers to choose from. Sports and fitness is a huge, varied industry. There are many different paths a person can take if they are interested in pursuing a career in this field. Some careers within the field overlap with other fields of interest too. For example, someone who has a love for sports but wants to make a career out of photography might pursue a position as a sports photographer. Or someone who has excellent communication skills might make a great public relations manager for a team.

Whatever path someone chooses, one thing can be certain: There will be a lot of time and work put into getting there. Like many careers, those in the sports and fitness industry often call for education or experience—and sometimes both. And much like the industry itself, there are plenty of options when it comes to which educational path to take. Some careers, such as those in personal training and coaching, don't require as much formal education. Instead, they might focus on specialized education or certifications, such as taking specific training courses or completing certifications in nutrition. Careers such as sports analysts or sports psychologists, however, may require higher education such as a postgraduate degree.

This book will explain some of these paths in greater detail. For now, here's a quick look at some of the careers within this industry:

- agents
- announcers
- athletic scouts
- club managers
- events managers
- gym owners
- nutritionists
- referees
- sports journalists
- sports photographers
- sports psychologists

CHAPTER TWO
Coaching

Coaches play an essential role in sports and fitness. Not only do they help teams strategize or help athletes better their game, but they also offer support and mentorship to athletes. Athletes and coaches often have unique relationships. Coaches take the time to understand each of their individual athletes' strengths, weaknesses, and which positions or roles they can play to best support the team. Coaches work to identify athletes' capabilities and needs to then pinpoint ways in which the athletes can improve upon weaknesses or hone strengths.

Middle School and High School Sports Coach

Think about which sports teams your school has and who coaches them. Middle and high school-level sports coaches have important roles in the lives of student athletes. If an athlete has a trusting, respectful relationship with their coach, the athlete will likely develop a stronger and more

Coaches are responsible for developing a team's skills, providing a strategic framework, and establishing a culture of positivity and sportsmanship.

positive relationship with the sport. Similarly, if a coach and athlete have a tense and difficult relationship, it can make for negative associations toward the coach and even the sport itself.

Some schools might not have the budget to hire full-time coaches. Most middle and high school coaches are teachers too. Although it's not always a requirement, it is common for coaches to have played the sport they coach at some point. At the very least, middle and high school coaches should have knowledge and a strong understanding of the game or sport.

Coaching school sports is a big commitment. High school coaches might spend about twenty hours a week on just their coaching positions. Add in their usual teaching responsibilities such as lesson plans and grading, and it's easy to see that coaches should be dedicated, hardworking individuals. People who want to be a coach should also have a passion for making a difference in young people's lives.

While it is possible to become a coach without any higher education, it is common for coaches to have a degree. If a coach is also teaching a subject such as English or history, they would likely have a degree more closely related to what they teach as well as a degree in education.

If a potential coach is not required to be a teacher as well, a school may have them log volunteer coaching hours. This allows the aspiring coach to get familiar with the team and to prove their passion and commitment to the game or sport. These coaches often have degrees too. Some of the common fields of study include sports science, kinesiology, physical education, and physiology.

Because of the higher risk of injury in sports and fitness than in other extracurricular activities, coaches are usually required to be certified in CPR and first aid. Middle and high school coaches should also possess traits such as strong leadership skills, patience, clear communication skills, and being goal oriented. These traits help coaches connect with and understand their players and the team and can help guide both the individuals and the team toward success.

The average salary for a middle or high school coach was $29,076 in 2024. The average salary for a middle or high school coach who also teaches was $48,114.

College Sports Coach

At the college level, coaches usually only work as full-time coaches. They are hired to train and work exclusively with a team. While the work of a high school coach and a college coach may be similar, the role of a college coach is more demanding. College athletic coaches analyze their athletes' performances to figure out strengths and weaknesses. They take extra time to study opposing teams to gain a better understanding of how to alter strategies for games or competitions. And most college coaches also take time to recruit athletes.

Most college-level coaches have earned a bachelor's degree. It's not unusual for college coaches to have also done some postgraduate work or to have second degrees as well. The top degrees are sports management and athletic training. Other common degrees include kinesiology, sports studies, coaching, and exercise science. Teams and athletes look to their coach for knowledge, expertise, and guidance. So in addition to a degree, it's important that coaches have strong leadership skills as well as excellent communication skills.

Aspiring coaches, especially of elite, high-ranking college teams, must have lower-level experience, such as acting as an assistant coach before becoming a head coach. Some may start off by coaching a youth or high school team or by working as an assistant coach at a college. Working as an assistant coach allows them to gain experience in everything from developing game day strategies to organizing practices. Assistant coaches usually have less responsibility than a head coach, but they can still play an active role in the progression and success of the team or of individual athletes.

In addition to college degrees, coaches at the college level are typically required to have various certifications. They are usually certified in CPR and first aid. Many college sports teams also require coaches to be certified by the National Collegiate Athletic Association. This means they can coach at colleges and universities that are part of the association. Some states might also require state-specific certification.

As of May 2023, collegiate coaches earned an average of $45,910 a year, with the top coaches earning more than $95,620. However, salary ranges depend on each coach's experience level, the school that employs them, their season record, and whether they work part-time or full-time.

Professional Head Coach

Much like college coaches, head coaches of professional sports teams are responsible for strategizing plays, analyzing opposing teams or players, and overseeing practices and games. However, unlike high school and college coaches, professional sports organizations often have teams of individuals to support a head coach. Those individuals might recruit new players, assist with training, and help with administrative tasks.

The steps to becoming a professional coach are a bit lengthier and require more than just education. It is not a requirement to have played college-level sports to be a head coach. Instead, most professional teams prefer coaches to have coaching experience at the college level. Successful pro coaches often have an established record of wins at the college level before moving on to professional sports. Because of this, becoming a professional coach often takes many years. Most head coaches of United States professional teams are in their mid to late forties or fifties when they take those positions.

The salary range of professional head coaches varies. For example, the National Football League pays head coaches millions of dollars, with the lowest paid coach receiving

Emma Hayes

Emma Hayes is the head coach of the United States Women's National Team (USWNT) for soccer. She has coached her way to the top of the game and is considered one of the best coaches in the world.

Hayes has coached for various teams in England and the United States, including the Arsenal Football Club Women's Team and the Chelsea Football Club Women's Team in London, England, and the Chicago Red Stars in Chicago, Illinois. Her longest coaching experience as of 2024 was with Chelsea Football Club Women's Team. She coached the club for eleven years before becoming head coach of the USWNT in 2024. She was inducted into the Football Association Women's Super League Hall of Fame in 2021 and holds seven league wins. Hayes also coached the USWNT to an Olympic gold medal at the 2024 Paris Olympics.

$3.5 million a year and the highest paid coach receiving $25 million a year. A pro coach's salary is based on factors such as number of wins and championships.

Strength and Conditioning Coaches

Athletes depend a lot on their bodies. They need to stay in peak physical condition to ensure they can perform at their best. This is where strength and conditioning coaches come in. Strength and conditioning coaches focus on keeping athletes in top physical condition. These coaches can work with all levels of athletes, from middle and high school

Strength and conditioning coaches help athletes develop sport-specific workouts that can lead to better performance and injury prevention.

to professional.

S&C coaches determine and guide strength training and conditioning training practices and exercises to meet different athletes' needs. Strength training focuses on activities that help build strength and power, such as body weight exercises including push-ups and lifting weights. These exercises increase muscle mass, strength, and power. Conditioning training focuses on activities such as running, plyometrics, endurance, and agility drills. Conditioning exercises can increase athletes' speed, agility, coordination, and cardiac health. When coupled together, strength and conditioning help keep athletes' bodies performing well by improving flexibility and overall performance and reducing risk of injury.

S&C coaches work with teams for group training sessions. They also work with individual athletes to address specific needs. They need to have extensive knowledge of both kinesiology and exercise science. They typically have a bachelor's degree as well as a certification in strength and conditioning. Certification should come from an industry-recognized program, such as the National Strength and Conditioning Association.

Additionally, to coach at the college or professional level, a master's degree is sometimes required. Common degrees for S&C coaches include kinesiology, exercise physiology, and physical education. S&C coaches might also need to complete a Level 2 fitness instructor course. These courses teach students how to be fitness instructors in gyms and health clubs. In addition to educational and certification backgrounds, S&C coaches should also have strong interpersonal skills and networking skills. Networking can open up the potential for different opportunities as well as allow the exchange of training methodologies and practices among other S&C coaches.

The salary for S&C coaches depends on what level and industry they work in. For example, entry-level S&C coaches can earn between $45,066 and $56,626. But senior-level coaches can earn between $132,000 and $165,000 annually.

CHAPTER THREE

Fitness and Wellness

Within the sports and fitness industry is an area known as fitness and wellness. It can include recreational gyms, specialized fitness centers, and nutritional information. Most aspects of fitness and wellness are to help the general population improve their overall physical health and well-being.

Gym Owner

Fitness and recreation centers, also known as gyms, are one of the most well-known and profitable areas of the sports and fitness industry. There are more than ninety thousand gyms in the United States. And as of 2020, the gym industry in the United States was worth $35 billion. Owning a gym can be exciting and rewarding. It can also be quite challenging. To own a gym, a person must have more than just a passion for fitness. They also need to understand business. Since a gym is a business, there are legal requirements that need to be met. Zoning regulations, health and hygiene standards, and business licenses and permits are just a few of the necessary elements a business owner must consider.

In addition to a love of sports and fitness, an aspiring gym owner should have strong leadership skills, excellent organizational skills, industry knowledge, and determination. Owning a gym does not require any special education. But it can be beneficial to have a strong background in both fitness and business or even a bachelor's degree or higher in business.

An aspiring gym owner has many factors to consider. The following are examples of questions to ask yourself if you think owning a gym might be an option for you:

- What type of gym do I want to open?
- What will the business plan be?
- Where will the gym be located?
- What will be the name of the gym?
- What are the startup costs?
- What types of equipment will be available?
- What types of classes will the gym offer?
- What will the membership pricing be?
- What kind of marketing will I utilize?
- What are the hours of operation?
- How many staff members will I need?

The type of revenue and income a gym brings in depends on a few factors. Some gyms are more successful than others. Franchise gyms are the most popular type of gym to open because they are considered the most profitable. These gyms are common ones you might have seen around your city and in others. They are sometimes called commercial gyms, and they cater to the general public and supply well-rounded equipment to meet the fitness and wellness goals of most people.

Some gym owners, however, prefer to open more specialized ones. In this category, CrossFit gyms are one of the most profitable facilities. Boutique gyms, which specialize in one or two types of fitness exercise, and yoga studios follow closely behind. Other types of specialty or boutique gyms include small group training, boot camps, gymnastics, Olympic weightlifting, and powerlifting facilities.

The average yearly revenue of gyms in the United States is $846,827. After paying for essential business needs such as employee salaries, lease payments, equipment upgrades or repairs, and more, the average gym owner takes home roughly $70,000 a year.

Personal Trainer

One of the most popular positions in the fitness industry is a personal trainer. According to the US Bureau of Labor Statistics (BLS), personal training is expected to grow by 14 percent between 2023 and 2033. This fast growth rate is because of an increase in businesses aiming to come back after gym attendance declined at the start of the COVID-19 pandemic, a desire for community building, and public awareness of health issues that personal training and exercise can help address, such as diabetes, heart disease, and obesity. More and more people are prioritizing their physical health and fitness.

Personal trainers are specialized trainers who meet one-on-one with clients or in small groups. They work to help people reach their fitness goals. Many personal trainers work at gyms and schedule appointments with their clients. Some

Personal trainers often lead small groups of people who have similar goals and fitness levels. These trainers build workouts tailored to their clients' specific needs.

personal trainers might own or rent a space in a facility. Some might travel to clients' homes for more convenience and privacy.

No matter where the personal trainer is working, their goal is typically the same: to improve the fitness levels of their clients. Some clients might be looking to improve their overall physical fitness. Some might be training for a specific goal. A personal trainer can help people achieve their goals by doing a few key things. First, they assess their clients' fitness levels, skills, and goals. Then, the trainer will create a personalized workout or training program for each client. Next, trainers help their clients learn and perform the exercises safely. They watch their clients perform exercises and then offer feedback or corrections as they go. Trainers then track their clients' progress and adjust their programs if needed.

Personal trainers are typically required to have a high

school diploma or general education diploma (GED). There is no college education requirement to become a personal trainer. But personal trainers are required to be certified. There are several certification courses available. Some of the most popular certification courses include those from the following:

- American College of Sports Medicine
- American Council on Exercise
- International Sports Sciences Association
- National Association of Sports Medicine

Personal trainers have the option to become certified in various specialties. These require specialized knowledge in different areas of fitness. Trainers can have more than one specialty certification. This can help broaden the types of clients they can help. Below are brief descriptions of some personal training specializations.

Bodybuilding trainers expand knowledge on how to work with, train, and coach competitive bodybuilding athletes. They combine knowledge of lifting, aerobic movements, and nutrition to meet clients' bodybuilding goals.

Corrective exercise trainers learn to work with clients who need improvement in their movement and posture. They look for and correct imbalances and dysfunction in the muscles, movement restrictions, and overall ability to move well.

CrossFit trainers, commonly referred to as coaches, teach clients proper exercise technique, form, and how to apply CrossFit methods to meet their clients' goals. They learn to work with diverse groups of clients and athletes.

Group fitness trainers lead group fitness classes and sometimes offer small group training.

Prenatal and postnatal fitness trainers gain specialized knowledge to help clients exercise safely throughout all stages of pregnancy and to exercise safely and recover post-birth.

Youth fitness specialist trainers learn different exercise guidelines for people between the ages of six and eighteen. They help young clients understand the importance of regular exercise and physical activity.

Aside from being certified, it is important for personal trainers to have excellent communication, customer service, and listening skills so they can better talk to and serve their clients. Personal trainers often help their clients push through challenging workouts and programs, so strong motivational skills are also important.

As of 2023, the average annual salary for personal trainers was $46,480. The highest 10 percent of personal trainers earned more than $80,740 annually.

Nutritionist

Athletes must take great care of their fitness levels to keep their bodies in top condition for athletic performance. But they also need to practice smart nutrition choices to fuel their bodies. That's where nutritionists come in. Nutritionists are people who specialize in helping clients with what they eat.

A variety of nutrition certifications and training are available. Each one plays a role in sports and fitness.

Certified nutrition coaches (CNCs) help clients improve their overall nutritional health by giving guidance and education on nutrition. The certification process includes

Interview with a CrossFit Coach: Sarah Tyler

What is your background in sports and fitness?

Prior to CrossFit, I have had very little experience in the sports and fitness world. I played softball for one summer when I was twelve years old and played in the marching band throughout high school.

How long have you been coaching CrossFit?

I started coaching in 2016 when I was thirty-four years old.

What certifications do you hold?

CrossFit Level 2 and USA Weightlifting Level 1.

How did you know you wanted to be a CrossFit coach, specifically?

I became very unhealthy after having my three kids. I went to the gym in search of a routine that would help me reach my fitness goals and would be fun to do! CrossFit helped me become more interested in what my body can do versus what my body looks like. I gained so much confidence in myself, and I desired to share that gift with others!

What does a typical day of coaching look like for you?

I write out my timeline of activities to make sure we stay on time, set up equipment, and plan a thoughtful warm-up. Classes are one hour long, and we typically have a strength workout and a cardio workout. I make sure I am demonstrating each movement for my class. I correct faults in movements, which is known as cueing. Cueing can be verbal, visual, and/or tactile. Each athlete learns differently, so it's important I show all types of corrections. I also make sure my class is enjoying their time with me. This is their happy hour!

What is the most rewarding part of your job?
There are two big things I love about coaching: Teaching people that they can do so many cool things that they may not have thought or believed they could do, and helping others learn new skills that unlock a love for sports regardless of age, gender, or body type.

What is the most challenging part of your job?
The most challenging part of coaching is having an athlete who is not easily coachable and/or someone who doesn't take their time in the gym seriously.

What is something that might be surprising for someone to learn about being a CrossFit coach?
It may be surprising that a coach, like me, got into sports and fitness later in life. I hold two American records in Olympic weightlifting, and I didn't start training in the sport until I was thirty-five years old. You don't have to be a lifelong athlete to become a CrossFit coach. You just need a passion for sports, an equal desire to teach others, and a continued desire for self-development.

If you could give advice to someone who might be thinking of becoming a CrossFit coach, what would it be?
Firstly, you have to love CrossFit and the methodology behind it. Secondly, you should have a desire to lead, help, and inspire others to do hard things! Naturally, when you inspire people to do hard things, they start believing in themselves and, in turn, go out into the world and inspire others.

studying the materials necessary and passing an exam. Aside from the certification program, it is not required for CNCs to have an educational background or extra training. CNCs can provide a general understanding of nutrition concepts, but they are not qualified to give specific eating plans or offer nutritional therapy advice.

CNCs help clients focus on lifestyle and behavioral changes around food. For example, a client has decided to begin eating a more well-rounded diet in addition to their workouts. But they aren't sure how to start. They ask the certified nutrition coach at their gym for guidance. The CNC gives general tips on how to adjust their eating habits. They might suggest to the client some healthful swaps to make, such as sometimes swapping out a nightly bowl of ice cream for Greek yogurt with fruit.

Gyms and fitness centers often employ CNCs. The coaches might work with personal trainers to offer advice to clients. Some personal trainers might even have their own nutrition coach certification to more effectively help their clients. CNCs might also work with schools, health-care companies, or wellness centers.

The average CNC salary range as of 2023 was between \$46,000 and \$75,000 a year. The income was based on experience level, marketing skills, number of clients, and location. Self-employed nutrition coaches—coaches who do not work with a gym or wellness center—tended to earn about \$10,000 more per year.

Certified nutrition specialists (CNSs) are similar to certified nutrition coaches. The major difference between a CNC and a CNS is their education. CNSs are considered advanced nutrition professionals. Their education focuses

Proper nutrition is an important part of health, but it can be overwhelming. Nutritionists, nutrition coaches, and nutrition specialists can help people understand their options and make the best choices for their needs.

more on the science behind nutrition. They also focus on how to use nutrition as a medical therapy.

Certified nutrition specialists can get jobs in hospitals, childcare facilities, school systems, institutions, clinics, and medical centers. Some CNSs might choose not to work with an employer and instead open their own private practice.

There are a number of requirements to become a CNS. It can be an intense process, but becoming a CNS establishes a person as an expert. The requirements to be a CNS are:

- minimum of a master's degree in nutrition or related health science
- one thousand hours of completed supervised practice experience
- passing score on the Certification Examination for Nutrition Specialists

The salaries for CNSs can vary widely. The amount can depend on factors such as experience, number of clients, and location. The average salary is $76,000 a year.

Sports nutritionists (SNs) are certified professionals who work with athletes of all levels. They use nutrition to improve athletic performance and overall physical health. An SN will take time to understand an athlete's specific needs. They might also create eating plans for athletes that will help get the most of their athletic performance. They are required to have a minimum of a bachelor's degree in nutrition or similar field. They must also complete a certification program and exam as well as obtain a license in the state where they plan on working.

Registered dietitians (RDs) are people who specialize in nutrition and diet. They work with people to improve their nutritional health. The difference between a CNS and an RD is that an RD can practice medical nutrition therapy. This means they can prescribe nutritional changes to help people cope with or manage certain illnesses or diseases.

Registered dietitians must go through several years' worth of education and credentials. These are the requirements for becoming an RD:

- bachelor's degree in nutrition or a related field
- completed dietetics program
- passing score on board exam
- state licensure or certification
- complete at least seventy-five hours of continuing education every five years

Registered dieticians can work in many places. They most often work in hospitals, schools, and food service organizations. As of 2024, the average pay range for an RD was between $71,000 and $100,000 a year. The average salary for an RD was $84,000 a year.

Sports Psychologist

Being an athlete is hard work. It is hard on a person's body but can also be hard on a person's mind. Some athletes might feel as if they need some extra help in this area.

A psychologist is a professional who studies and treats mental health conditions and behaviors. Sports psychologists are professionals who help improve the mental well-being of athletes. Maintaining their mental health can help an athlete maintain and improve their performance. Sports psychologists learn all they can about the motivational aspects of sports and fitness as well as the connection between mental health and sports performance.

Sports psychologists also help athletes set goals. They might help them improve their self-confidence or self-esteem, especially in the game or sport. They can help athletes with conditions or concerns such as eating disorders, depression, burnout, career transitions, and more. Taking care of one's mind is not only for athletes. Coaches and other sports professionals can also benefit from sports psychology. For example, coaches can get help with things such as team building, motivational tools, and leadership skills.

Some common aspects sports psychologists may help with include:

- increasing focus to minimize anxiety
- practicing mental preparation
- practicing visualization techniques
- handling fears related to athletic performance
- recovering mentally from sports-related injuries
- coming up with effective training routines

It takes many years to complete the required education and training to become a sports psychologist. The following are the recommended steps to do so.

Bachelor's degree: The Association for Applied Sports Psychology says that "students may be best served to major in psychology or kinesiology and a minor in sports, exercise, and/or performance psychology."

Postgraduate degree: Most positions require a doctorate, but others may require only a master's. The most common areas of study for a master's degree include sports psychology, counseling psychology, or clinical psychology. For doctorate degree options, a doctor of psychology degree, typically in sports psychology, allows someone to work directly with people. This degree is best for those who want to work with athletes or coaches. A doctor of philosophy focuses more on research. This degree is better suited for those who wish to teach or do research—in this case, within sports psychology.

Postgraduate experience: You must complete two years (or about three thousand hours) of supervised experience in the form of internships, master's practicums, or employment.

State licensure: Each state has different requirements for licensing, but most require a doctoral degree and two years of supervised experience as well as passing a board exam.

Board certification: Board certification helps psychologists provide better care and shows their clients that they're experts. To be certified by the American Board of Sports Psychology, you have to have a doctorate in psychology, complete training that the board mandates, score at least 80 percent on the certification exam, and complete seventy-five athlete assessments (equal to about 750 working hours).

The salary for sports psychologists depends on variables such as location and years of experience. As of 2024, the average salary for a sports psychologist was about $105,000 per year.

Physical Therapist

Injury is a common issue in sports and fitness. It's likely to happen to most athletes at some point in their career. While some injuries might be quick to heal and bounce back from, others might need more recovery.

Physical therapists are professionals who help athletes recover from injuries. They also work with athletes to prevent future injuries. Physical therapists use stretches, exercises, massage therapy, and other types of physical movement to help patients recover. To help prevent injuries, they might also have athletes work to improve mobility, strength, and range of motion. Common athletic injuries and issues they might help with include:

- anterior cruciate ligament (ACL) tears
- joint dysfunction
- knee injuries
- ligament tears
- muscle strains
- rotator cuff tears
- tendinitis

Becoming a physical therapist can take up to seven years of education and training. To become a sports therapist, a person must earn a bachelor's degree, especially in kinesiology, exercise science, health science, biology, or psychology, and then a doctor of physical therapy degree. They must also receive state licensure where they plan to practice. Additional certification is not required but can earn someone more job opportunities. It typically requires at least two thousand hours of clinical experience and a passing score on a certification exam.

Many physical therapists work in places such as hospitals, surgery rehabilitation centers, nursing homes, schools, medical clinics, or private practices. But there are many university and professional sports teams that have their own physical therapists too.

A physical therapist sees many people in one day and should have strong physical stamina. They should enjoy physical activity and be able to spend most of their working days moving. People who want to become physical therapists should also have traits such as compassion, respect for others, communication skills, and time management skills.

Physical therapy can be a taxing but rewarding career. The average salary for a physical therapist was between $72,000 and $130,000 as of 2023.

CHAPTER FOUR

The Other Side of Sports

When it comes to professional sports, there are also teams of individuals who help keep things running behind the scenes. They might design the stadium or facility. They could help promote special events. Or they might help select the team of players. This side of the industry can appeal to those who have other passions in addition to sports and fitness.

Talent Scout

Have you ever wondered how a person becomes a player on a professional sports team? Or how college sports select their athletes? Talent scouts watch and choose players for teams. They observe athletes to judge and rate their abilities, skills, statistics, and overall potential. Then they decide which athletes would be a good fit for the team.

Before scouting a game or event, talent scouts research some of the athletes they are going to watch. They study their statistics and game history. They even pay attention to how athletes interact with their teammates, coaches, friends, and family. Scouts need to make sure that the athletes they are recruiting fit the team overall, not just athletically.

Talent scouts usually work for specific colleges or professional teams. They often search all over the country and sometimes the world to find great athletes. Most scouts spend weeks or even months traveling. They fly, drive, and ride buses or trains, all in search of talented athletes. When they find athletes they feel would work well with the team, they recommend them to the team manager or organization. Sometimes they might offer an athlete a position right on the spot. In these cases, they might also need to do some contract negotiations.

Talent scouts should have certain skills to help them do their jobs well. They should be sociable and comfortable interacting with many different people from various backgrounds. They should also be able to communicate clearly and excel at negotiating with players and coaches. Talent scouts must also have strong analytical stills and a clear understanding of sports statistics. Finally, they must be experts in the sport they are scouting and have a deep knowledge of its rules, unique characteristics, and any challenges associated with it.

The requirements for becoming a scout can vary depending on where the person works. But having a bachelor's degree in a sports-related field is often preferred. Some degrees that are helpful in this career include sports management, sports science, and kinesiology. While having past sports experience is not a requirement, having experience in the sport you scout can be beneficial. As of 2023, a professional talent scout could make up to $51,000 per year.

Sports Photographer

Many people working in sports and fitness get into the industry because it is their main interest or passion. But some people might have more than one passion or interest, and some might believe that wanting a career in sports and fitness means having to neglect those other interests. The reality is that there are career paths that can combine two or more interests. Sports photography is one of those careers. If you find yourself torn between a career in photography or a career in sports and fitness, then perhaps being a sports photographer might be up your alley.

Sports photographers are exactly what they sound like. They take photos of athletes, teams, games and competitions, and more. These professionals might work for a magazine, newspaper, or online publication. They might work independently as freelance photographers. Or they might be regular staff members for an agency such as Getty Images, which provides images for various forms of publishing—including this book!

Sports photographers can work within many sports and a variety of areas within them. Many choose sports such as basketball, football, or soccer. Some might choose to photograph skiing, horseback riding, or swimming. Working in a variety of sports means working in different settings. Photographers might also have to work in bad or extreme weather conditions. This means photographers might need special equipment and clothing to keep themselves and their cameras and lenses safe from the weather.

The right equipment is important for a sports photographer. Being able to capture important moments during a fast-paced sporting event is the key to success in this job.

Photographers use a lot of special equipment. Many professional photographers use multiple cameras and lenses for one game or event. Photographers typically pay for their own cameras and equipment. But this may not always be the case. A photographer who is on staff with an agency or organization might have their equipment provided, although that is rare. But freelance photographers are always expected to provide their own cameras. Since photography equipment can be quite expensive, aspiring sports photographers should keep this expense in mind.

Like other professional photographers, having a degree is not a requirement. There are many professional photographers who do not have degrees. Instead, they make up for it with their talent and experience. However, having a college degree can help set you apart from the competition. Sports photography has many technical skills, so even though there is no education requirement, it can be very helpful to take some photography classes or courses. You can find photography programs at community colleges, universities, and online.

While specific education is not required, a strong portfolio is. A portfolio is a small collection of a photographer's best work. It is a way to show potential employers or clients their skills and photography style.

Sports photographers need to understand more than just photography. They also need to understand the sport they are photographing. For example, if a photographer is taking photos at a gymnastics meet but does not know anything about how a meet is organized, they might miss some key photo opportunities. Photographers also need to be able to work quickly and efficiently. They must always keep their eyes peeled for interesting angles, lighting, and moments that might become the next incredible sports photo.

These photographers should also have skills and traits such as quick reaction time, attention to detail, strong technical and sports skills, networking skills, and adaptability. This will help them identify and capture clear photographs and connect with the people they're photographing. They might have to carry around a lot of equipment for many hours, so having stamina and strength may also be beneficial in this field.

The median salary for a sports photographer in 2024 was $59,000. The pay range can vary depending on location and experience. The pay range for sports photographers is between $44,000 and $79,000 a year.

Sports Journalist

Have you ever seen sports news headlines such as "Home Team Makes Remarkable Comeback in Final Minutes of a Game" in print or online? Or maybe you've heard highlights of sporting events on the news. Sports journalists write these articles and reports. They are professional writers and reporters who write about all things sports.

Some sports journalists might focus on highlights of games. Others might write feature stories on key players. Sports journalists write everything from play-by-play analyses to investigative stories. They research the topics that they are assigned and interview people who might have information or opinions on the topic. Then they write the story or article and review it for accuracy, grammar, and style. Sometimes information might change after an article or story is published. When this happens, the journalist might have to make updates to the information.

Sports journalists work for many types of publications. They might work for an online newspaper or magazine. They might work for a local news station. Some even get to work for big sports entertainment companies such as ESPN or *Sports Illustrated*. Many journalists work as permanent staff members, but some might work as freelance journalists.

Like other types of journalists, becoming a sports journalist requires a mix of education and experience. They need a bachelor's degree, preferably in journalism or a related field such as English or communications. Often, they must complete an internship at a newspaper, broadcast station, or other organization that puts out sports news. Experience on a high school or college newspaper or other publication will also help prime their skills.

Similar to photographers, journalists typically use portfolios to help them get jobs. A journalist's portfolio includes examples of their published work as well as other writing samples that might demonstrate their strengths. This gives potential employers a chance to see what their skills and style are like.

Journalists should have communication skills, interviewing skills, research skills, and creativity. They should be able to work well under pressure and stick to quick, strict deadlines. They should also have some technological skills, such as being able to use coding software to publish their stories and articles. As of 2024, the average salary range for sports journalists was between $41,000 and $77,000.

Sports Analyst

You might not realize it, but the world of sports involves a lot of math and statistics. Sports analysts are professionals who interpret data and analytics to understand and make decisions about the sports industry. They can use data to analyze teams and players. These valuable insights can help give a competitive edge to an individual athlete or a team.

Sports analysts can work for broadcast channels such as ESPN or NBC. They might give insight into player and team performances as well as coaching decisions during a sports broadcast. They might also work directly for sports teams. These analysts use data from training and practices to help improve player and team performance. The data they analyze covers a wide range of variables including athlete and team playing statistics as well as physical fitness levels, how and

Playing Moneyball with Billy Beane

Billy Beane is the former general manager of the Oakland Athletics. He managed the team from 1997 until 2015. In addition to being the youngest general manager in the history of Major League Baseball, Beane changed the way baseball teams chose athletes. How did he do this? With sports analytics.

Beane used an approach known as Moneyball. He analyzed data and statistics to find players that had the best chance of performing well. *The Sport Journal* notes that Beane's "main two statistics included on-base percentage and slugging percentage. These two stats combined to form a new statistic called on-base plus slugging." And it worked.

Beane's approach was so successful that in 2002 it helped the Oakland Athletics have one of their best seasons in the team's history. The baseball team won twenty consecutive games that season. They had gone from being one of the worst teams in the league to making it into the postseason playoffs. In 2003 Michael Lewis wrote a book called *Moneyball* about Beane and his unique approach. In 2011 that book was turned into a hit movie of the same title.

when players get injured, and even ticket sales.

Some analysts might even work directly with coaches. The data that sports analysts evaluate helps coaches learn where athletes and teams might need to improve and where their strong points are. Some sports analysts might also work for podcasts, media companies, or even for sporting goods manufacturers. Sports analysts can also play important roles in tasks outside of games such as improving fan engagement and coming up with new products.

You might have guessed that to become a professional sports analyst, you need to have a strong background in math and statistics. Typically, sports analysts are required to have a bachelor's degree. Math and statistics are the most common specialties. Sports analytics, sports management, and business analytics are other degree options for those wanting to be sports analysts. The pay range of sports analysts varies, with the lowest being $31,000 and the highest being $130,000 per year as of 2024. The average was $73,261.

Sports Engineer

Engineers are trained professionals who solve problems and create new things. They use math, science, and technology. But what does that have to do with sports and fitness?

Sports engineers are professionals who design, test, and apply new sporting equipment, clothing, and more. The title of sports engineer covers a broad range of job descriptions and duties. Some might work on new sports ball designs, improved helmets or other safety equipment, or specialty performance uniforms or clothing. They also design things such as turf on football fields and arenas and stadiums.

In order for sports engineers to do their job well, they have to pay close attention to details. When designing new equipment or clothing, they study the way an athlete's body moves. They notice things such as the way a ball bounces, at what angle a foot strikes the ground, and much more. Sports engineers who design structures such as arenas and complexes must consider how many fans should fit inside. They might need to think about the way sound travels or how weather

How to Get Started

If you want to have a career in the sports and fitness field, you might consider how you can take steps to prepare. Getting involved in sports and fitness is a great way to do so. Here are some different ways to gain experience and build skills to help you get started in the sports and fitness industry.

Volunteering

Check with local teams and sporting organizations to see if they need volunteers. Some organizations may need help with logistical tasks. Volunteers might change scoreboards, maintain equipment, sell tickets, organize events and tournaments, and more. If you have an interest in coaching in the future, you can also check with youth teams, such as Pee Wee or Pop Warner football and Little League baseball teams, as well as amateur teams, such as community recreational leagues, that may need assistance.

Internships

Internships are a great way to gain experience in the field you are interested in joining. Internships are short-term positions with organizations and companies. Not only do internships show employers that you're serious about your interests and ready to learn, but they can also help you figure out what you like and don't like about a job.

Although internships are commonly unpaid positions, they allow for firsthand learning that can help you gain knowledge and experience in your chosen professional path. They are excellent experiences to add to your résumé. Most internships are only available to college students. They show potential employers that you have taken the initiative to learn new skills and meet people in the industry. This might help you stand out against other applicants when applying for jobs. Many professional sports teams and organizations offer summer internships for positions in business operations, social media and marketing, finance, technology, legal, sponsorships, and more.

Network

Networking can play a significant role in your career path. The more people you are in contact with in the field you are working toward, the better chance you have of hearing about an opportunity that could be right for you. Some of the ways you can network are:

- joining student or community organizations
- participating in summer or after-school programs, teams, and more
- utilizing your school or local community college's career center
- getting involved in sports journalism through local newspapers, magazines, and broadcasting networks

Participate

Taking part in sports and fitness might be obvious for those who want to become professional athletes or coaches. Being on a school team or club is an easy way to gain hands-on knowledge about sports and fitness. But participating in the sports and fitness industry can go beyond playing a sport. For some, it might be taking part in fundraising, marketing, or promotions. For others, it might be applying to be a team's game day photographer. Some might prefer writing up their own journalistic reports for the school or local paper. Or maybe they help teach younger players the rules of a new sport or game.

might affect the field or turf. Because of this, sports engineers should be detail-oriented and able to think about situations and problems from many different angles.

Becoming a sports engineer is not a straightforward process. Some employers might have different requirements than others. And sometimes there are highly recommended but not necessarily required degrees or training requirements. Here are some common requirements to become a sports engineer:

- bachelor's degree in mechanical engineering, physics, medical physics, or sports medicine
- master's degree (recommended)
- sports technology certification (highly recommended)

Similar to many other careers, the average salary for sports engineers varies depending on location and experience level. As of 2024, the upper range was between $91,000 and $161,000 a year, and the average salary was $87,891 a year.

Sports Marketing Manager

Have you ever seen someone wearing a shirt or hat with a sports team's logo on it? Have you ever seen a commercial for a big game or event such as the Olympics or the Super Bowl? Those are examples of sports marketing. It is a way to promote a sport or sporting event, a team, an athlete, or products such as branded clothing, accessories, or equipment. Sports marketing plays a huge role in bringing in money and growing relationships with fans.

Sports marketing involves understanding who is watching and listening to a sport and providing an experience that meets their needs.

A sports marketing manager is in charge of promoting, or marketing, a team, athlete, or gym. Sports marketing managers can work with major, well-known brands as well as small businesses. For example, a gym owner might want more people to know about their grand opening. They hire a sports marketing manager to post on social media. The marketing manager works with the owner to figure out their needs. The marketing manager might also put ads in the local newspaper and give out free water bottles with the gym logo on them. This is all marketing. Larger teams or organizations conduct advertising on a bigger scale such as with billboards or commercials, as well as host special promotions such as ticket giveaways.

Sponsorships are another way that sports marketing managers help teams, athletes, or organizations. Sponsorships are when a team, athlete, or event partner with a brand or company. Usually it means that a brand will send promotional items such as clothing and equipment to an athlete or team. The more the athlete uses those items, the more people will see them. This leads to more people recognizing the brand. The athlete or team gets equipment it may need, and the brand gets more promotion. Sports marketing managers are the ones to coordinate these win-win agreements.

Sports marketing managers typically need a bachelor's degree. Common areas of study include marketing, advertising, business, and public relations. Sports marketing can be a difficult industry, so it is advised to complete an internship or two to get experience, which employers often like to see in job candidates. A master's degree is not required but can help a candidate stand out too.

Similar to many other careers, the average salary range for sports marketing managers can depend on where they live and what experience they have. As of 2024, the pay range was between $80,000 and $145,000 a year, with an average of $76,922.

The careers in this chapter are just some of the many jobs available within the sports industry. From social media specialists for sports teams to ice resurfacing drivers for arenas, there are careers for people with all types of interests and specialties.

CHAPTER FIVE

The Future of Sports Careers

Overall, the future of the sports and fitness industry looks promising. The BLS reports that all occupations in the industry are expected to grow faster than the average between 2023 and 2033. The average growth rate for most occupations is 4 percent. The BLS expects jobs in sports medicine and athletic training to grow the fastest. These are the areas that are expected to have above-average growth through 2033:

- sports medicine (or physical therapy): 14 percent
- fitness trainers: 14 percent
- athletes and competitors: 11 percent
- umpires and referees: 10 percent
- coaches and scouts: 9 percent
- dietitians and nutritionists: 7 percent

Many different factors impact the sports industry's growth. One is that women's sports are making a big impact on the industry. Women's sports saw a huge increase in attendance, viewers, and media rights between 2023 and 2024. Exciting young athletes, better marketing for women's sports, more investment in women's teams, and increased media coverage have earned leagues such as the Women's National Basketball Association, National Women's Soccer League, and Women's Hockey League many new fans. Women's sports fans also tend to be younger and have more expendable income. This means there is likely to be even more of an increase in fan investment. And with more interest and investment in women's sports comes more career opportunities.

Another factor in the growth of the industry is that athletes as well as other people are getting even more interested in fitness. There is a stronger emphasis on overall fitness and well-being, including mental health. This opens up more opportunities in this field for trainers, gym owners, and more.

AI and Sports Technology

The sports and fitness industry is constantly changing. New innovations, new jobs, and plenty of growth opportunities are happening all the time. One of the biggest changes is advances in technology.

It is no secret that technology plays a big role in almost every aspect of our lives. Many industries have been impacted both positively and negatively by technology, and the sports and fitness industry is no different. But sports and tech might be a promising pair that could bring even more career opportunities to the industry.

Some of the newest trends in technology have found

Personal fitness devices that sync with smartphone apps can provide athletes and fitness enthusiasts with data to help them reach their goals and set new ones.

their way into sports and fitness. Artificial intelligence (AI) is experiencing rapid growth. In sports and fitness, AI is used in various ways. One is in wearable technology. Devices with AI can track performance metrics and can give feedback to the people wearing them. The technology in these devices can track heart rate and find potential weaknesses or strengths in athletes' performance, such as their speed. It can even use the information to create new training plans. AI can also be used

A Growing Market

According to the research company Grand View Research, the global sports analytics market in particular is growing at an incredible rate. In 2023 this market brought in $3.52 billion. And it is estimated to only keep growing, with an expected investment increase of 21.5 percent between 2024 and 2030. This growth is due to the increase in advanced technologies used in sports such as in sports data analytics, in digital signage in stadiums meant to attract more fans, and in infrastructure.

Analytics in soccer especially are helping this increase because the sport is so popular both in the US and globally. In fact, the soccer portion is expected to have the highest growth rate at 23 percent.

to create game or competition scenarios that athletes might experience in real life.

AI can also help judges, referees, and other sports officials make better calls during competitions. For example, competitive gymnastics uses an AI-assisted system for scoring. It uses high-definition cameras to record and analyze the movements gymnasts perform. The system records the movements in 3D, which helps judges more accurately score the performance. According to *Forbes*, AI in gymnastics "is helping reduce human error, provide consistency in evaluations, and help eliminate human emotions in scoring."

According to the Business Research Company, the global AI sports market is expected to grow by 28.8 percent between 2024 and 2028. So what does the integration of

AI in sports and fitness mean for career outlooks? Some people may argue that the role of AI hurts the job market in the industry. AI can be used in a variety of ways, including to analyze data or to come up with marketing campaign concepts. This opens the possibility of lowering the need for human employees. But in reality, AI often helps create demand for new roles within the industry. This is most noticeable in sports analysis. A 2024 study found that the use of AI technology "could lead to a shift in the type of jobs available in the industry, with more emphasis on data analysis and less on traditional marketing skills."

Plus, although wearable devices increasingly rely on AI to collect data, that data still needs to be analyzed and interpreted by a person. Because of this, there has been a growing demand for data analysts in the industry, specifically those with the skills to interpret the data provided by AI.

CONCLUSION

An Industry for All

There are so many paths a person can take to be part of this industry. From coaching young players to being a sports photographer, there is a career for practically everyone. Maybe you feel more drawn to the more common sports and fitness careers, such as personal training. You might love the idea of being a writer but can't seem to tear yourself away from your love of sports, so maybe being a sports journalist is the right fit for you. Whatever way you decide to be involved, sports and fitness careers are exciting and are hardly ever the same day-to-day.

After reading this book, you might have a better idea of what type of sports and fitness careers interest you. You can explore your interests even more by taking steps now to help you prepare for one of these careers. You could interview a local athlete, volunteer to help coach your younger sibling's recreational games, or take photos of you and your friends playing different sports. There are a lot of fun ways to get started on your future career. Sports and fitness is a growing, varied industry that has plenty of career options for people with all kinds of skills and interests.

One of the most important aspects of the sports and fitness industry is building relationships—between players and coaches, trainers and clients, and athletes and their fans, just to name a few.

GLOSSARY

analytics: a field of computer science that uses math and statistics to find meaningful patterns

anxiety: a feeling of unease, tension, worry, or fear

certification: the process of earning an official document proving a status or achievement

credential: a qualification showing that someone is suitable for a job position

disciplined: being able to control the way one works, lives, or behaves to achieve a goal

elite: superior in quality or rank

expendable: easily replaced, used up, or consumed

freelance: independent; not affiliated with an organization or company

infrastructure: foundation and basic structure

interpersonal: having to do with relationships or communication between people

kinesiology: the study of movement

licensure: granting of professional permissions to practice in a particular field

marketing: promoting and selling products, services, or business through advertising

networking: interacting with others to develop professional or social contacts

nutrition: the branch of science that deals with nutrients and food necessary for physical health and growth

plyometrics: a type of exercise that uses fast, explosive movements to improve speed, power, and strength

portfolio: a collection of professional examples that showcase one's skills and qualifications

postgraduate: the course of study taken after completing a bachelor's degree

recruiting: enrolling someone into an organization or team

resilience: the ability to recover quickly from obstacles or difficulties

revenue: the total amount of money brought in over a set amount of time

startup: a newly established business

undergraduate: a college or university program that leads to an associate's or bachelor's degree

SOURCE NOTES

6 "The global sports . . . billion by 2023.": Research and Markets, "Sports Market Opportunities and Strategies to 2033: $862.6 Billion Industry Analysis by Type, Revenue Source, Ownership, Region, and Company," Yahoo Finance, May 21, 2024, https://finance.yahoo.com/news/sports-market-opportunities-strategies-2033-081600019.html.

9 "You got this. It's your time.": Megan Sauer, "Simone Biles Tells Herself These 3 Words Before She Competes—Everyone Should Try It, Ivy League-Trained Expert Says," CNBC, August 2, 2024, https://www.cnbc.com/2024/08/02/simone-biles-tells-herself-3-words-to-get-ready-to-compete.html.

32 "students may be . . . and/or performance psychology": "Undergraduate Programs in Sport, Exercise, and Performance Psychology," Association for Applied Sports Psychology, accessed September 30, 2024, https://appliedsportpsych.org/students-center/undergraduate-programs/.

42 "main two statistics . . . on-base plus slugging": Ehren Wassermann, Daniel R. Czech, Matthew J. Wilson, and A. Barry Joyner, "An Examination of the Moneyball Theory: A Baseball Statistical Analysis," *The Sport Journal*, January 2, 2005, https://thesportjournal.org/article/an-examination-of-the-moneyball-theory-a-baseball-statistical-analysis/.

52 "is helping reduce . . . emotions in scoring": Kathleen Walch, "How AI Is Revolutionizing Professional Sports," *Forbes*, August 16, 2024, https://www.forbes.com/sites/kathleenwalch/2024/08/16/how-ai-is-revolutionizing-professional-sports/.

53 "could lead to . . . traditional marketing skills": Dag Ø. Madsen, Paulína Mihaľová, Gábor Géczi, Alexandra Mittelman, and Bojan Jorgič, "Artificial Intelligence Development and Dissemination Impact on the Sports Industry Labor Market," *Frontiers in Sports and Active Living* 6, (2024): 1363892, https://www.ncbi.nlm.nih.gov/pmc/articles/PMC11007172/.

SELECTED BIBLIOGRAPHY

Anani, Zak. "Employment Trends in the Global Sports Industry." Global Institute of Sport, September 18, 2024. https://gis.sport/news/employment-trends-in-the-global-sports-industry/.

Grey, Sheryl. "How to Become a Sports Psychologist: Salary, Education Requirements and Job Growth." *Forbes*. Updated October 7, 2024. https://www.forbes.com/advisor/education/psychology-and-counseling/become-a-sports-psychologist/.

"How to Become a Sports Nutritionist: All You Need to Know." Husson University Online, February 14, 2024. https://www.husson.edu/online/blog/2024/02/sports-nutrition-jobs.

"How to Break into Coaching and Sports Administration Careers." Tulane University School of Professional Advancement. Accessed September 13, 2024. https://sopa.tulane.edu/blog/how-break-coaching-and-sports-administration-careers.

Kassouf, Jack. "The Story Behind USWNT's Coach at the Olympics, Emma Hayes." ESPN, July 25, 2024. https://www.espn.com/olympics/story/_/id/40621125/the-story-uswnt-coach-olympics-emma-hayes.

Whittle, Matt. "How to Become a Nutritionist: Everything You Should Know." *Forbes*. Updated January 30, 2024. https://www.forbes.com/advisor/education/science/how-to-become-a-nutritionist/.

Yellowbrick. "The Remarkable Career of Billy Beane." Yellowbrick, October 15, 2023. https://www.yellowbrick.co/blog/sports/the-remarkable-career-of-billy-beane.

FURTHER INFORMATION

Books

Careers: The Ultimate Guide to Planning Your Future. 3rd ed. New York: DK, 2022.
This book helps guide teens and new graduates in choosing a job or career path.

Loureiro, Stephanie. *Engineering a Win.* Ann Arbor, MI: Cherry Lake, 2024.
This book explores how engineering has improved athletic performance, facilities, and equipment.

Loureiro, Stephanie. *Strategic Statistics.* Ann Arbor, MI: Cherry Lake, 2024.
This book discusses the use of sports statistics and analytics in various areas of professional sports.

Morkes, Andrew. *Exploring Engineering Careers.* Minneapolis: Twenty-First Century Books, 2026.
This book explores various career options for those interested in engineering.

Swanson, Jennifer. *The Secret Science of Sports: The Math, Physics, and Mechanical Engineering Behind Every Grand Slam, Triple Axel, and Penalty Kick.* New York: Black Dog & Leventhal, 2021.
This book helps break down science and math concepts, such as gravity and algebra, and explains how different sports use these concepts.

Websites

American College of Sports Medicine: Resource Library
https://www.acsm.org/education-resources/trending-topics-resources/resource-library
This website includes books, articles, videos, and more for people to learn about exercise science and sports medicine.

Britannica Students: Sports Industry
https://kids.britannica.com/students/article/sports-industry/277186
This page examines the history of the sports industry, how much it's worth in the United States, and more.

Careers in Sports and Health: What Jobs Are Possible?
https://www.apu.apus.edu/area-of-study/nursing-and-health-sciences/resources/careers-in-sports-and-health/
From American Public University, this article looks at more careers in the sports and fitness industry and potential degree paths.

NBC Sports
https://www.nbcsports.com/
This website includes sports highlights and news for a variety of professional and college sports.

Occupational Outlook Handbook
https://www.bls.gov/ooh/
Run by the US Bureau of Labor Statistics, this website allows you to search and find information such as experience and education requirements, pay rate, and growth outlook on various careers and jobs.

INDEX

American College of Sports Medicine, 24
American Council on Exercise, 24
artificial intelligence (AI), 50–53

Beane, Billy, 42
Biles, Simone, 9
broadcast, 40–41

certified nutrition coach, 25, 28
certified nutrition specialist, 28–29
coach, 4, 6, 12–17, 19, 24–26, 28, 54
college, 4, 8–10, 14–16, 19, 26, 35, 39–40, 44–45
CrossFit, 22, 24–27

degree
  bachelor's, 15, 19, 21, 30–31, 34, 36, 40, 43, 46, 48
  doctoral, 33
  master's, 19, 30, 32–33, 46, 48
  postgraduate, 11, 15, 32–33
  undergraduate, 10

engineer, 43, 46
England, 17
ESPN, 40–41
exercise science, 15, 19, 34

Football Association Women's Super League, 17

general education diploma, 24
Grand View Research, 52
gymnastics, 22, 39, 52
gyms, 6, 19–22

Hayes, Emma, 17
high school, 9, 12–17, 23–24, 40

International Sports Sciences Association, 24
internship, 33, 40, 44–45, 48

journalist
  sports journalist, 7, 11, 40–41, 54

kinesiology, 10, 14–15, 19, 32, 34, 36

Major League Baseball, 42
mental health, 31–32, 50
Moneyball, 42

National Collegiate Athletic Association, 15
National Football League, 16
National Strength and Conditioning Association, 19
NBC, 41
nutrition, 11, 26–31
nutritionist, 4, 27

Oakland Athletics, 42
Olympics, 9, 17, 46

personal trainer, 22–23, 26
photography, 10–11, 37–39
physical education, 14, 19
physical therapist, 4, 34
physiology, 14, 19
professional, 6–9, 16, 18–19, 31, 34–38, 40, 43–45
professional athlete, 6, 8–9
psychologist, 4–5, 31–33

recovery, 33
referees, 7, 11, 49, 52
registered dietitians, 30, 49
research, 32–33, 35, 40–41, 52

scouts, 7, 11, 35–36, 49
Sports Illustrated, 40
sports management, 15, 36, 43
sports nutritionist, 30
sports science, 14, 36
strength and conditioning, 4, 17, 19

Tyler, Sarah, 26

wearable technology, 51, 53
women's sports, 49–50

ABOUT THE AUTHOR

Stephanie Loureiro is a freelance writer and editor. When she's not writing, she loves reading, lifting weights, singing loudly to Taylor Swift, and spending time with her husband, daughter, and their two dogs.

PHOTO ACKNOWLEDGMENTS

Image credits: ruizluquepaz/E+/Getty images, p. 5; SDI Productions/E+/Getty Images, p. 7; miodrag ignjatovic/E+, p. 8; South_agency/E+/Getty Images, p. 13; Cecilie_Arcurs/E+/Getty Images, p. 18; SolStock/E+/Getty Images, p. 23; ruizluquepaz/E+/Getty Images, p. 29; dlewis33/E+/Getty Images, p. 38; courtneyk/E+/Getty Images, p. 47; Guido Mieth/Stone/Getty Images, p. 51; SolStock/E+/Getty Images, p. 55.

Cover image: The Good Brigade/Digital Vision/Getty Images